A Night of Lullabies

Selected and Illustrated by

SARAH POOLEY

LIMITED EDITIONS
BOOKTITLES

Early to bed
Early to rise
Makes a man
healthy, wealthy
and wise.

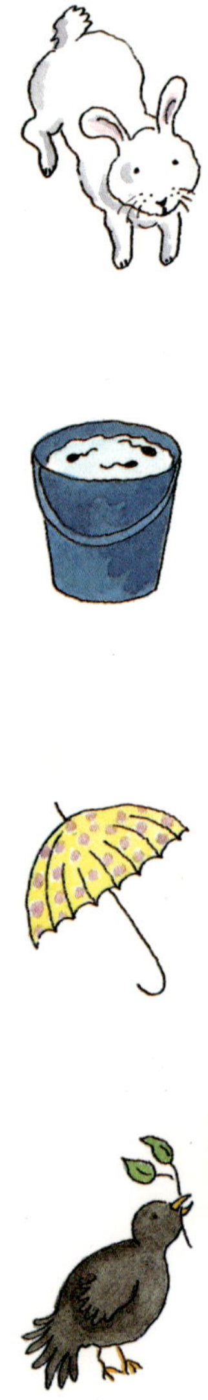

To bed, to bed
Says Sleepy Head
Tarry awhile says Slow
Put on the pan
Says Greedy Nan
we'll sup before we go.

As I was going up the stair
I met a man who wasn't there
He wasn't there again today
How I wish he'd go away!

Up the wooden hill to Blanket Fair
What shall we have when we get there?
A bucket full of water and penny worth of hay . . .

Rub-a-dub-dub
Three men in a tub
And who do you think they be?
The butcher, the baker
The candlestick maker,
Turn them out, knaves all three.

Here is the sea, the wavy sea
Here is the boat and here is me
All the little fishes down below
Wriggle their tails, and away they all go.

This little pig had a rub-a-dub
This little pig had a scrub-a-scrub
This little pig-a-wig ran upstairs
This little pig-a-wig called out, Bears!
Down came the jar with a loud Slam! Slam!
This little pig had all the jam .

Little man in coalpit goes
Knock, Knock, Knock,
Up he comes, up he comes
out the top!

Comb my hair said Lady Fair
And put some grease upon it
Not too much of the nasty stuff
Or you'll spoil my nice new bonnet.

It's raining, it's pouring
The little old man is snoring
He went to bed with a bump on
his head
And didn't get up in the
morning.

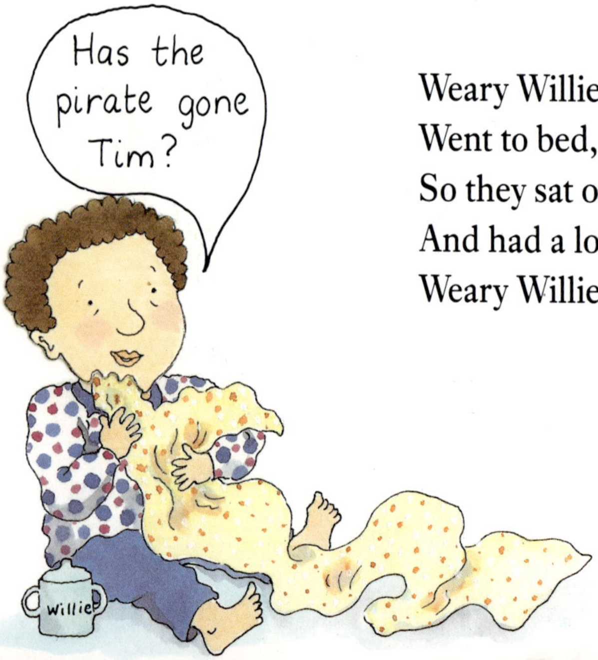

Weary Willie, and tired Tim
Went to bed, but they couldn't get in
So they sat on the ground
And had a look around –
Weary Willie and Tired Tim.

Red sky at night, shepherds' delight
Red sky in the morning, shepherds' warning.

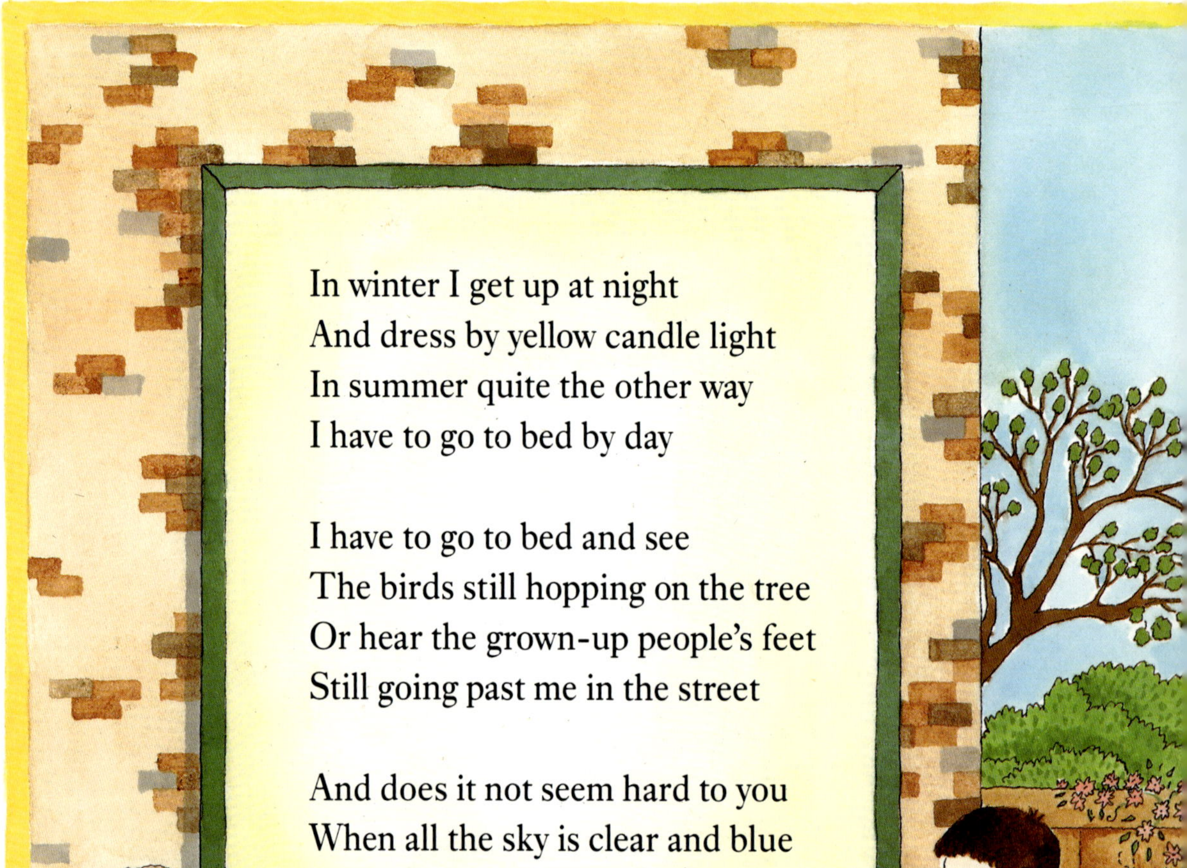

In winter I get up at night
And dress by yellow candle light
In summer quite the other way
I have to go to bed by day

I have to go to bed and see
The birds still hopping on the tree
Or hear the grown-up people's feet
Still going past me in the street

And does it not seem hard to you
When all the sky is clear and blue
And I should like so much to play
To have to go to bed by day?

Kiss me quick
Nice evening!
sniff

Go to bed first
a golden purse
Go to bed second
a golden pheasant
Go to bed third
a golden bird!

When all the cows were sleeping
And the sun had gone to bed
Up jumped the scarecrow
And this is what he said
I'm a dingle, dangle scarecrow
With a flippy, floppy hat
I can shake my hands like this
and shake my feet like that
When all the hens were roosting
And the moon behind the cloud
Up jumped the scarecrow
And shouted very loud . . .

Wee Willie Winkie runs through the town
Upstairs and downstairs in his nightgown
Rapping at the window, crying through the lock
Are the children all in bed, for now it's eight o'clock.

Boys and girls come out to play
The moon doth shine as bright as day
Leave your supper and leave your sleep
And join your playfellows in the street!
Come with a whoop and come with a call,
Come with a good will or not at all.
Up the ladder and down the wall
A half penny loaf will serve us all
You find milk and I'll find flour
And we'll have a pudding in half an hour.

In jumping and tumbling
we spend the whole day
Till night by arriving
Has finished our play

What then? One and all
There's no more to be said
As we tumbled all day
So we tumble to bed.

Trot, trot, trot,
Go and never stop
Trudge along, my little pony,
Where'tis rough and where'tis stony,
go and never stop
Trot, trot, trot, trot, trot!

Here is the ostrich straight and tall
Nodding his head above us all
Here is the long snake on the ground
Wriggling upon the stones he found
Here are the birds that fly so high
Spreading their wings across the sky.

Here is the hedgehog prickly small
Rolling himself into a ball
Here is the spider scuttling around
Treading so lightly on the ground
Here are the children fast asleep
And here at nightfall owls do peep.

Round, and round the garden
Like a teddy bear
One step, two step
Tickle you under there!

There was an old owl who lived in an oak
The more he heard the less he spoke
The less he spoke, the more he heard
Why aren't we like that wise old bird?

Hey diddle, diddle
The cat and the fiddle
The cow jumped over the moon
The little dog laughed to see such a sight
And the dish ran away with the spoon.

Dance to your daddy
My little babby
Dance to you daddy
My little lamb

You shall have a fishy
In a little dishy
You shall have a fishy
When the boat comes in

You shall have an apple
You shall have a plum
You shall have a rattle
When your daddy comes home.

One fine October morning
In September last July
The moon lay thick upon the ground
The snow shone in the sky
The flowers were singing gaily
And the birds were in full bloom
I went down to the cellar
To sweep the upstairs room.

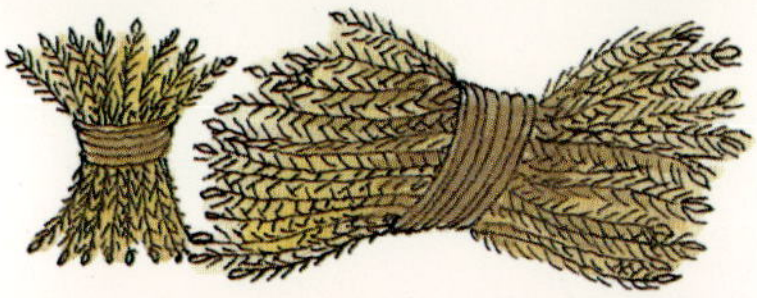

With my little broom, I sweep sweep sweep
On my little toes I creep creep creep
With my little eyes I peep peep peep
On my little bed I sleep sleep sleep.

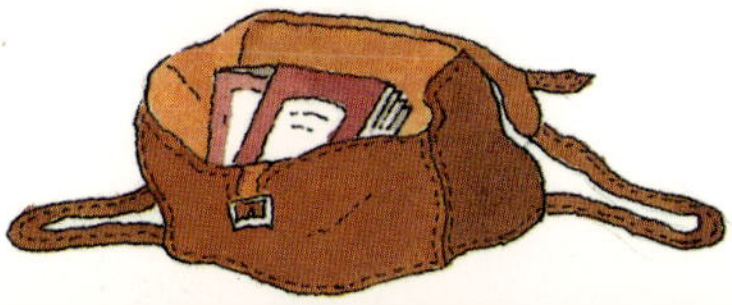

Hey-how for Halloween
All the witches to be seen
Some black and some green
Hey-how for Halloween .

The Man in the Moon as he sails the sky
Is a very remarkable skipper
But he made a mistake when he tried to take
A drink of milk for the Dipper
He dipped it into the Milky Way
And slowly and carefully filled it
The Big Bear growled and the Little Bear howled
And scared him so that he spilled it!

There was an old woman
who made green cheese
By beating up spinach
and curds with a spoon
And when she had done it
with very great ease
Tossed it up to the sky
and declared 'twas the moon.

To sleep easy all night
Let your supper be light
Or else you'll complain
Of a stomach in pain.

O Timothy Tim
Has ten pink toes
And ten pink toes
Has Timothy Tim
They go with him
Wherever he goes
And wherever he goes
They go with him

O Timothy Tim
Has two blue eyes
And two blue eyes
Has Timothy Tim
They cry with him
Whenever he cries
And whenever he cries
They cry with him

O Timothy Tim
Has one red head
And one red head
Has Timothy Tim
It sleeps with him
In Timothy's bed
Sleep well red head
Of Timothy Tim .

Rock-a-bye baby on the tree top
When the wind blows the cradle will rock
When the bough breaks the cradle will fall
Down will come baby, cradle and all .

Sleep baby sleep
The father watches the sheep
The mother is shaking the dreamland tree
And softly a little dream falls on thee
Sleep, baby, sleep.

Golden slumbers
Kiss your eyes
Smiles await you
When you rise
Sleep little baby
Don't you cry
And I will sing a lullaby.

El Coqui sings a sweet song at twilight
He is singing as sleep comes to me
When I wake all alone in the moonlight
El Coqui sings goodnight from the tree
Co-qui, Co-qui, Co-qui, qui, qui, qui .

Here are the lady's knives and forks
Here is the lady's table
Here is the lady's looking glass
And here is the baby's cradle .

Monkeys in the forest
Beggarmen in rags
Marrow in a Knucklebone
Gold in leather bags

Dumplings in the oven
Fishes in a pool
Flowers in a parlour
Dunces in a school

Feathers in a pillow
Cattle in a shed
Honey in a beehive
And me in bed.

It was a dark and stormy night
And the captain said to Antonio
Tell us a tale Antonio . . .
And this is the tale Antonio told
It was a dark and stormy night
And the captain said to Antonio
Tell us a tale Antonio . . .
And this is the tale Antonio told
It was a dark and stormy night
etc.

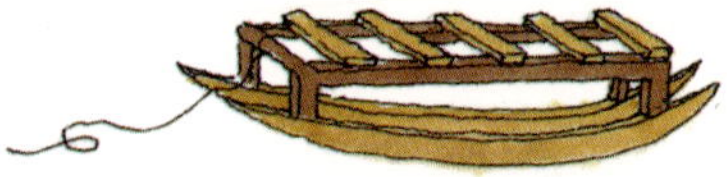

Softly, softly falling snow
This is how the snowflakes go
Pitter, patter, pitter, patter
Pit pit pat
Down go the raindrops
On my hat .

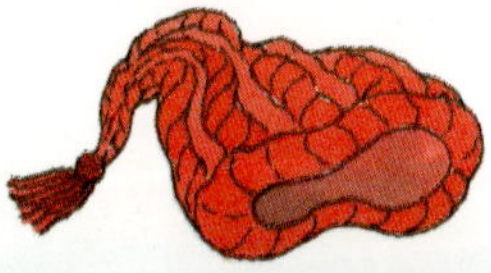

Silent night, ho-ly night
All is calm, all is bright
Round yon vir-gin mother and child
Ho-ly infant so ten-der and mild
Sleep in hea-ven-ly peace
Sleep in hea-ven-ly peace .

Away in a manger, no crib for a bed
The little Lord Jesus laid down his sweet head
The stars in the bright sky
Looked down where he lay
The Little Lord Jesus asleep on the hay.

Little Jesus, sweetly sleep, do not stir
We will send you a coat of fur
We will rock you, rock you, rock you
We will rock you, rock you, rock you
See the fur to keep you warm
Snugly round your tiny form.

Star light, star bright
First star I've seen tonight
Wish I may wish I might
Have this wish I wish tonight.

Twinkle, twinkle, little star
How I wonder what you are
Up above the world so high
Like a diamond in the sky .

Jellicle cats come out tonight
Jellicle cats come one and all
The Jellicle Moon is shining bright
Jellicles come to the Jellicle Ball

Jellicle cats are black and white
Jellicle cats are rather small
Jellicle cats are merry and bright
And pleasant to hear when they caterwaul
Jellicle cats have cheerful faces
Jellicle cats have bright black eyes
They like to practice their airs and graces
And wait for the Jellicle Moon to rise . . .

One, two, three, four o'clock, four o'clock rock
Five, six, seven o'clock, eight o'clock rock
Nine, ten, eleven o'clock, twelve o'clock rock
We're gonna rock, gonna rock around the clock tonight
Rock around the clock tonight
We're gonna rock, rock rock till broad daylight
We're gonna rock, gonna rock around the clock tonight!

The clock
Ticks
The clock
Tocks
This way,
That way,
And never never
Stops
Tick-tock
Tick-tock
Tick-tock.

As soon as I'm in bed at night
And snugly settled down
The little girl I am by day
Goes very suddenly away
And then I'm Mrs Brown

I have a family of six
And all of them have names
The girls are Joyce and Nancy Maud
The boys are Marmaduke and Claude
And Percival and James

We have a house with twenty rooms
A mile away from town
I think it's good for girls and boys
To be allowed to make a noise
And so does Mr Brown

We do the most exciting things
Enough to make you creep
And on and on and on we go
I sometimes wonder if I know
When I have gone to sleep.

Au clair de le Lu-ne, Mon a-mi Pier-rot,
Prê-te moi ta plu-me. Pour e-crire un mot.
Ma chan-delle est mor-te, Je n-ai plus defeu;
Ou-vre moi ta por-te, Pour l'amour de Dieu.

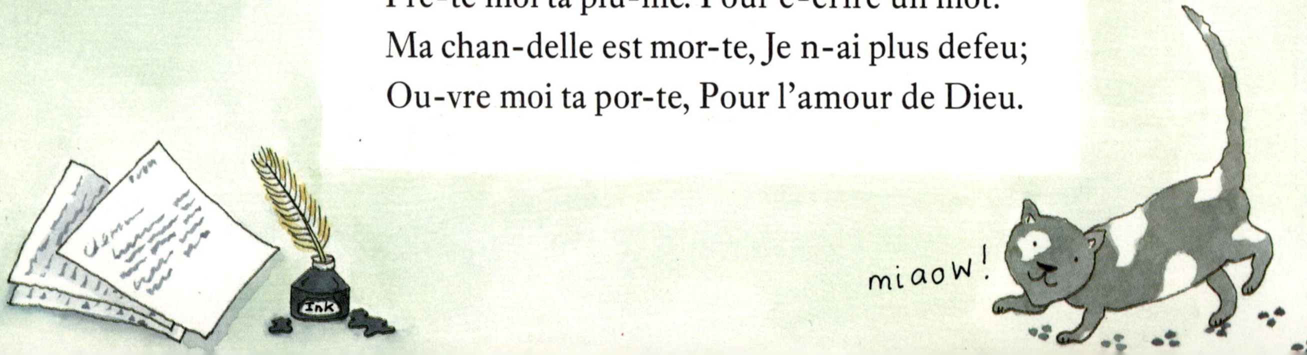

If I were a bear,
And a big bear too,
I shouldn't much care,
If it froze or snew;
I shouldn't much mind
If I snowed or friz —
I'd be all fur lined
With a coat like his

For I'd have fur boots and a brown fur wrap
And brown fur knickers and a big fur cup
I'd have a fur muffle-ruff to cover my jaws
And brown fur mittens on my big brown paws
With a big brown furry-down up to my head
I'd sleep all the winter in a big fur bed.

From Breakfast on through all the day
At home among my friends I stay
But every night I go abroad
Afar into the Land of Nod

All by myself I have to go,
With none to tell me what to do —
All alone beside the streams
And up the mountainsides of dreams

The strangest things are there for me
Both things to eat and things to see
And many frightening sights abroad
Till morning in the Land of Nod

Try as I like to find the way
I never can get back by day
Nor can remember plain and clear
The curious music that I hear.

INDEX OF FIRST LINES

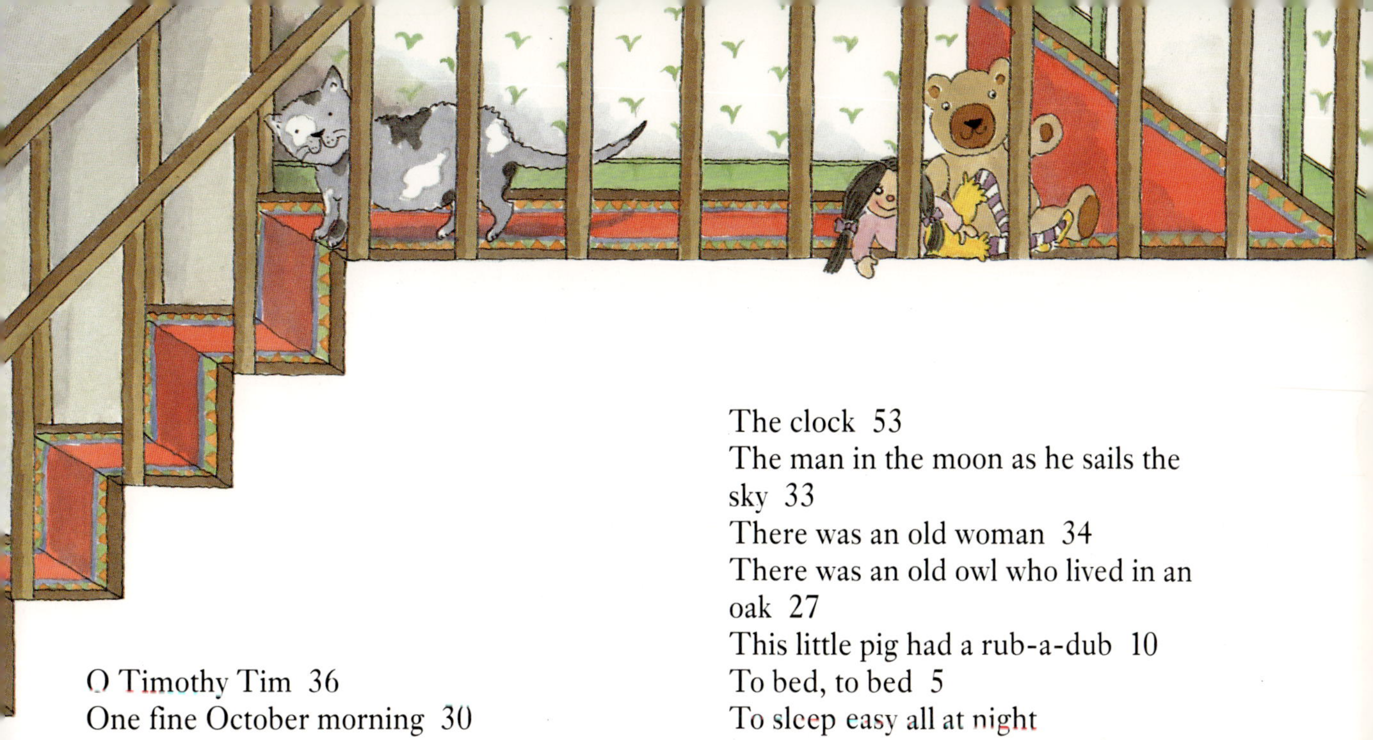

ACKNOWLEDGEMENTS:

Mrs Brown: courtesy of The Society of Authors as the literary representative of the Estate of Rose Fyleman.

Here is the ostrich straight and tall: Elizabeth Matterson originally published in NURSERY RHYMES AND FINGER PLAYS: Boyce & Bartlett

With my little broom I sweep, sweep, sweep: Elizabeth Matterson originally published in NEW NURSERY JINGLES: E Barnard Books

Rock Around The Clock – written by Max Freedman & Jimmy De Knight © 1953 Myers Music Inc. for the World, used by kind permission of the Edward Kassner Music Co. Limited (U.K. representative)

The Jellicle Cats from OLD POSSUMS BOOK OF PRACTICAL CATS by T. S. Eliot by kind permission of Faber and Faber Ltd.